My Reef

JOHN WILKINSON was _____ up on the Cornish coast and on Dartmoor. After university at Cambridge he trained as a psychiatric nurse and worked in mental health services and public health in the West Midlands, South Wales and London's East End. In 2005 he moved to the United States and has held academic positions at the University of Notre Dame and at the University of Chicago where he is currently a Professor in the Department of English and Director of Creative Writing. His extensive publications include a selected poems (*Schedule of Unrest*, 2014). Wilkinson has held Fulbright and National Humanities Center fellowships.

My Reef
My Manifest Array

John Wilkinson

CARCANET

First published in Great Britain in 2019 by
Carcanet
Alliance House, 30 Cross Street
Manchester M2 7AQ
www.carcanet.co.uk

A CIP catalogue record for this book is
available from the British Library,
ISBN 978 1 78410 691 1

Book design by Andrew Latimer
Printed in Great Britain by SRP Ltd., Exeter, Devon

The publisher acknowledges financial
assistance from Arts Council England.

Acknowledgements

Certain of these poems have been published previously, usually in different versions, in the following journals whose editors I gratefully acknowledge: *Blackbox Manifold*, *Botch*, *Chicago Review*, *Cordite Poetry Review*, *Hambone*, *PN Review*, *Poetry*, *Verge*, *Verse Version* (with Chinese translations by Zhao Gu), *The Wolf*, *#NewWriting* – and in the anthology *Atlantic Drift* edited by James Byrne and Robert Sheppard (Arc Publications and Edge Hill University Press 2017). 'Self Defeated' was published as a broadside by Constitutional Information, Sheffield, 2014. My thanks to Sam Ladkin and Sara Crangle. I thank Srikanth 'Chicu' Reddy for his encouragement and his unmatchable collegiality. Jessica Stockholder, Patrick Chamberlain, Judith Farquhar and James Hevia have done much to make Chicago my other home. Thank you to the National Humanities Center for hospitality in 2017–18, and to Jo McDonagh and Colin Jones for Poets Road. And home is where Maudie is.

Contents

On the Destruction of Temples

I.

Elder blossom with its stench,
strict reek of geraniums,
fair are the insouciant drapes
behind which creatures scoot.

Lightning anneals its cleft air,
there can be no ambiguity;
wine is tapped from blossom,
fecund sun must cast light.

Be as the unread blood insists,
as light-sensitive cells,
rents in the rose scent tagged
by twitching skirmishers.

Lip-scanners, touch parsers,
catalogue the sunshine's mottle;
deer hid in the complex,
fragrant streaks, act petrified,

being cognisant, nerved to bolt —
their patchwork awning, air's
now fitful cries, scarcely
shades the panicky creatures.

Piece them out. A loaded runic
yearns to kill, and its dire
stalking, night-time creeps of
purpose scope and dissect.

2.

Squint chisel pares to the quick,
blocks of music in the ear
stay inert until time's rush
from bloated gutters, lash

against storm windows, slew
through veined clerestories,
sheets of water, living
torrents o'er-brim the cistern –

are you composed still, are you
hungry still at your plate,
do you select an automatic
flower from its braced stalk,

dreamer whose fluidity
shifts the block of Lyonesse?
Beyond its portals lies a forked
infarct once was twitching,

latterly a table laid with tables
where a head betimes lay,
trig points punctuate its slope-
aspect, fields of soft 'x's

won't be pledged or disavowed,
suppliance has at it, heads
nod and bury in that erst-
fluting marsh, serrated beaks

prod the verges drying bated
sense harsh scour, last
efforts brace palings kissing
numbers open each as Jesse's

rod fluoresces over its parallels.
Rails stretch, planks climb,
bars curl at access points.
Number-franked fleeces spoil

pegged out stiff as a board.
May domains a dreamer spills
shawl earth with spheres,
melt solids, drench accord.

3.

Where did the despoiled
invest time clung to, to resettle
haunt workings? Squatters
riddle at the grate, disfiguring

its chrome with hurried embers,
cumulus in puffs of palest
blue is forcing through sectors,
white stone is seething,

smooth white stone is seething
as a circular saw bites,
iconoclasts trim an
alabaster nimbus, dismantle.

What of the silica cues
forwarding to their devices,
fingers catch on winking stars –
what of graphite grass square

or storms of bells crossing slate
and clay tablets, aggressive
trees and virulent entabled
mosses? Now traffic lights

at named intersections
take aim, 'Do Not Enter' boxes
fill with caustic, lenses zoom,
the safe vacuities of recall

drift in stone cisterns
imageless and drained, rue
stains the borders dreamt
touch suffices to corroborate;

the bled will take their time
literally, express the juice
from marrowbones, papyri,
lathering over unburied names.

4.

Dissolve a stain impress a tadpole grid
       prevent belligerent frogs
from slithering foam ladders, clench
       hypothesis of day or fibre-
glass Parthenon, slot stone by stone
       to face a blue imperative façade,
held back by a fretful lightweight
       summer force, a failing state,
clapperboard soon trounced in dis-
       array to fault that perpending
Hebrew, Aramaic star, its earth-lit
       psalmody first greeted them
in pause halfway, where each explores
       his body lit on a target screen,
a selfie in a failing state articulates
       through its positions, army
veterans click heels, occupy the leaden
       bearing set and biocast, die-
cast in miniature, a clatter from the
       medium now more specified
investigated life-forms, spasms of a
       green too eventful and a red
back to base, a rucked cloud drops
       hollow rounds on a signaller
squats low, who wriggles into mud,
       braids lines that click and pop,
fendillates before the wires, death
       on his crawl board, cellulose
ladders roll in front of cloud and clod.

Menhirs grow exacerbated shadows
thrown across the barbed
wire like pads of ticking I swarm over.

5.

Fracturing while desert wind is veering
        sand in wadded streams, an ever-
motive idol's craquelure moves to speak:

Lava bulges, rock waves, sand's shrill
        deliverance, skirl of seed
strews a swept floor, bends oaken stands.
        Your model God may fix his
steroid face on blank despondency,
        whitewashed Eden and the pews
levelled, noble truths smash images
        smitten into unreflective
marvellous lofty, struck eyes blanked
        girls amid their downtown
valediction, glaze a solstice hollowed
        for its rubble, cratering the siren
murk, spawning into gaped pent-
        vocatives loofa car, full-page
sheds and shacks, roofed slalom
        custody behind-the-scenes
sandstone brows bullets furrow, hew
        to horizontal rungs, vapour
tray wasps and dayflies get sorted,
        rack of heaven, brilliant contrails
marking up the blue, their payloads
        crash down on cracked cheeks,
stretch to this, stretch to children
        huddled in such famished state
goaded over canted splurge of chalk
        towards their image blank-eyed.

Motivated impact prints the preacher
on his blanks, he self-prates
blank sheet, a clean start, a ruled page.

6.

Invite the details, detail found missing,
    give more details, bunched
flies combed apart, toil in furrows
    hunched under crows' avidity
spilling out on space, for space
    has enticed them, no bread to eat
or clean water, fragile backs braced
    against the curve of rarefaction
lever blocks and ties of marble or jarrah,
    memorialise or making tracks
bruise the open source so as then gush,
    thus will a corporate raider
keep his promise, thus will he certify
    larders of stiff worms, and at a v
bidirectional but snapping-to
    on the elusivest charge, this
way or that laying out in dot dot dot
    the pleonastic offer yet more
brought to the table free of regulation,
    snuff this haunted air, decrying
air that cannot guide or train an
    eye that needs its sight lines
or ear that wants air transposed:
    The pilgrims while diminished
choose trekking over flat bright
    faces, clinging to the handholds,
slopes of carrara slide them to a drop
    dizzy can't avoid the gaping
gorge of a server keeps in its domain
    all detail, hutch of secret names.

Risen effigy, worked from clitter strewn
in your wake, attract sunken
stars, abstract the geode fists upwards.

7.

Stone supplants a breathing pasturage,
　　boughs droop with heavy
lambency, a circlet of silver water knots.

Stone lays its shadow under elevations,
　　shadow for a populace to settle,
in their settlements the earth warms,
　　lungs quake, a heart judders.
Streaks of mitosis took the strong path
　　of oversight might have felted
fruit flies into galaxies so thick
　　their lope vastness would have
birthed between species, brought close
　　in humming birds and
lemurs, sneak prions, brilliant cars
　　condensed to their one flock,
piped into projected stainless channels
　　rampant throughout abattoirs,
while on its steel circlet rows back
　　the devastated ark, up shit creek
without a paddle, choked with mists,
　　where still are promulgated
variant gaseous bodies, oscillations
　　a domestic slave harkens to,
no quittance other oboe double reed
　　curls out of sighing, dying strings
recombine in sudden surge: arise,
　　a puff of vapour, an explosion
might have been a theatre, stain
　　mayhap auditorium, shadow
creeps above a warm still convivial fold.

Universal droplets and thunder
writing chewed into pellets fall
　　upon a stone cascade, birthing,
blast the heads off birdseed stalks,
　　sodden match heads, figurines.

8.

Aggressively its digits blanch through
    tarry billows, bold bollards rot,
cuttlebones, feathers, polystyrene
    feign to swim, fly, hover, weigh,
and the reserved space disintegrates
    to flotsam. Having so been buoyed,
life rapid as a switching current tip-
    tingles. Inventory of light-blocks
tumbles on the film set like Nimrud,
    avalanching extras upward
once disposable they made their stand
    shadow wash across each
others' imprints, such as they, faint,
    and in their superimposed breasts
expressive light shows through a pulse
    of one dense proposition, n,
this note scored for true temper or a
    quantity precisely tuned degrade
ladder upsampling, scrabbling angels
    sprawl across each other's
entrails exposed as a shrimp's guts,
    anteing until the last, anteing
funicular to ride the swaying marble,
    ocean sectors split out of a
glacier, how will a smashed statue
    in 3D restoral count its beads,
failing state divided by a grid coalition,
    gnomonic map projection grips
over tribal lands, ice fields loomed on
    by an idol's shadow swept away.

A yellow butterfly visits heavy blossom.
    Bees rise and fall on airy
plummets. Tables of law flit cancelled.

9.

Haul down ladders, sure larval pulses
        flush cells dying bleed
colour out of brain and distant colonies.

        Deep in the trenches music fails,
mud submerges herds of intellectual
        dapple. What of the living stone
in that? whips, fans and feathers stirring
        damselflies and spermy bloom
on airways chamfered overhead,
        knit bones to keep aloft our necks;
foresight of enduring lizards
        threads through vertebrae with
fovea-to-finger optic spasms,
        grinding out old tunes. Earth
mutters in her mine workings, angry
        ocean growls back and forth
peopling reefs, reefs which blanch,
        stone deprived of thought decays,
feldspar disintegrates, half-vacant
        palaces of column coral, gonad
pebbledash engulfed with needles,
        nautilus armadas wake to goad
thunder-struck clocks, to spawn at dusk.
        Weigh on these, white grass
pressed by human biomass, pressed
        by dream excrement, a grassy
arborescence but whose splayed roots
        soaking on the pavement of grey
postwar precincts, presses down,

shellacking hard floating
cysts, insects and our stray thoughts,
coral cities decompose to sand
flush with sunset and what once was.

10.

No clean slate although wiped
with microfibres, shadow
writing will persist – no
clean slate we can indict: day

cracks its bland blue mouth,
and on the fresh sheet bullet-
holes, addresses glower,
deeper grooves continue under

new-twitching tendrils, lit
ploughlines left by conquerors.
In empty courts yells echo,
stone splits into lancets,

insect squadrons are glancing
off windows that explosion
cured restless sand into,
re-inscribing hieroglyphs,

rotted pearls, translucent china,
imitation gems, gold chains,
saturating tissues carmine,
tapers of our human wax.

All may dream of wipe-out,
dream impeccable scrubs,
dream an undegraded
skin, fingers yearn to look into,

serpents slither out of nostrils,
curl on smashed arches,
hiss in niches eyes introduce –
no clean slate, no clean slate:

Tyrian red will be extracted
out of murex, carmine
smashed from cochineals,
concentrating blood and nerves,

black manganese in circuit,
channels sooting thick
blue assumption, YInMn
sky powdered, aniline blue WS.

II.

Tuned uniquely for near field,
no depth, minimal throw,
this source for colour splinters
into cats-eyes, orb artefacts:

purple flares, soon to fringe
apparent black and white,
cut blocks are molten. Stock
having been prepared, press

where spangles, this patch of
tissue on the roughened
silver bark, on first approach
speculative – chances are

accepts the graft. So nerves
send their unsheathed, disem-
bodied fibres arcing
through air's warmth, signals

tightly packed in carbon tubes,
which crude daub, blanco,
vantablack will slather,
straying from receptor sites.

Brutally you rasp the stock,
cut to insert a wiry stem.
Blips cascade, hair's-breadth
lines are crossing. 'The drops

are insular', but insularity
breaks and re-sets
figuring light, sends viral
ducts threading into gratings.

12.

Churning cloud, a wafer screen
froze but its prolific
snipped threads dangle summer-
long through blue distress;

billowing holds blue at bay
beneath slomo streamers,
shallow moor that staples down
convulsive, combative earth,

sends tillers and tin miners
flush from moor to inlet,
where loaded waves are cupped
between steep-sided jetties

clouded over; although stars
lose their likenesses, they spill
from every mouth unheard,
long sigh, a body's blue vapour.

Colour-cast disintegrates, sticky
tar thins out: deep-down
optic tentacles had writhed,
paths would skirt full brooks

through holly, mint, adders-
tongue and fern, negotiating
beech and hazel copse: chancery
of winds had ruffled and the

stands of mallow softly swayed,
fish skittered between sandy
melts — such lather fades,
abandoning the field to blue.

Skimming the surfactant,
consciousness gives up a ghost,
blue guzzles the moon jelly,
blue vaunts its own incipience.

To Coralize

What more than winter hath that dire art found,
These purple currents edged with violets round
To coralize, which softly wont to slide
In crimson wavelets, and in scarlet tide?
RICHARD CRASHAW

I.

An oil of a kind invents a sky over this obdurate surface.
Once again to enlist the chattels. Pooling
half the kingdom cloudily concealed then made visible

expels these from their caves, cold water flats, jail,
winkled out of tins. Lining up for judgment, authorised
or damned, fitted to their faith cloud while carnival

decorates the streets, the almost gendered word stops,
rocking on a tongue. Time to redeem. Cheers,
yet contemplation fails the rumpled and more beautiful

shot silk. Through storm shall whirl quicken and
all sorts were sheep and goat triage. Quietly though tip.
Oil pools on granite, proof against the lithic standstill.

Epiphyte! Blaze on the arm! Lacklustre your scaly trunk!
Sprout madly his incisions. Shower scent
on forest floor needle-packed, over circling animals,

tuft magdalenic boughs with rose and cabbage mutants
colour-drained. This is not equivalent. Scorned
every high-sided cot, their slop chest flashes midday.

Is that how you like it, gaping from mere gravity,
blow-up hanging out to dry? Flip phantom on his heels,
tainted to the uppers, kicking through base clouds.

And this again. God-given and our pre-approved,
its vestments drag upon the present peg and so lacerate.
Blood requires no lesion, evidence no spurt wounds,

choice point ladders, eels and frogs break surface
wrinkling screens in loud celebration, pooling
round his shoes whose carnal contents are made visible.

2.

Such was red tide the crested
masters of the town rode,
proudly on their stakes
hammered down, silvering

with dawn-effect, the helms
of gulls and pelicans,
'wrong thoughts', they taunt,
repeat their gagging order,

stultify the deaf music, call
this luminescence gilds
a seamy underbelly,
tracks and restores shoals'

steel-locking manifold; such
instruction at the harbour
leaks its fine slick oil,
to back-flow over mewling

green carcass. How it shakes
silently and eloquently,
turned over to expose
a universal deep structure

surfacing that now congeals,
lurid lunar rides
thick microorganisms. Blot:
a trustworthy linear supply –

Smudge: complex circuit.
Cries twist among the poles,
painfully responsive to
red shadows' draw and lure.

3.

Some lose the stomach, sick
glow wans them in the face
slowly lapping; at the
quayside pluck and vorticle

get ironed out, classical
once broken from the mouth,
pockmarks of desire less
compelled yet further lessen;

surface tension shatters into
swirl by use of a deciding
stake – corruption
subteraqueous might shoal.

Is that the basal boom I hear?
Is that Caliphate?
The Thousand Year Reich,
G7, where it convokes?

Stability they seek is staring
back tantamount,
will not pacify the face
cross-sectioned for analysis –

the spirit dies in lithographs
stacked in microns-deep
wafer over wafer, revives
dint of turbid squall:

what else but usual rain
published on the closed sea,
eliciting its opposites in
bubbles clustering like roe,

spits on airy counterparts,
resolves into one form,
shapes into a looming
kraken between sea and sky.

4.

You get this call cuts its
auger flight: pigeons amble
amid mirages and poke
sunshine limescale,

one flurrying at sight of its
own shadow, hears polar
earth attract. Sediment plugs
whizz between macrocells.

You get this follow-up:
heaps of chain along a quay
run through human lading,
'stay on line,' 'don't pull out'.

The sea is turning in its sleep,
dawn copies, copy that.
Its reconstructed shrilling
net covers Portland ME.

5.

They're going belly-up, glow
with putrefaction, their stink
torments neutral air
wrapped round the quay,

as though a taproot, dragon-
tree whose function
crusted with dry heaves,
thrusts prismatic out of shale,

its flame throws out opal,
opal seeps milk, milk welling
eyes with opacity, one opal
eye mirrors one diaglyph –

it stinks totally. What wind
will blow off vapour, catch
petrol winking rivers
dressed in peacock foulness,

blow pink, yellow and blue
obsolete paper records
sorted in a ladder system?
The ladder lays down flat,

angels flash activity lights,
rungs activate like sound bars
laying out their falsehoods
for roads to cross marsh,

carbon on their underside,
their upper sides of crimson
reek with fevered
volatility from stage to stage:

up and down, down and up,
governed by the return pump
which from below supplies
brackish sink holes.

6.

Convolvulus or auger
twist for their little plugs
of euphoria – triple
hissy fit will spark their fire,

after-shave, sal volatile,
vodka fire that rip through
lamp/ temple/ grove,
licking at the deckle edge

enveloping the slick seen
blistered on far ocean,
to glint in Freda's circlets
up her arms – infant tendrils

etching little curls in sand,
breeze in convolutions
thinking fits right into,
circles would pin down.

Twisting bodies draw
home her breath, crunch
animal swarf submissively,
uplifted by their psalms

say what they have to say:
Mouths foam at metal bars,
clips, hair-slides, roses
twitchily let loose

so as to finger amulets,
bloom where anti-mother
freed from her blood,
invites with reek and fire.

7.

Leaf miner, scaly moth,
pierce this feldspar but stay
with odd attachment,
rooted in the warm

porous wall and warm
porous sky. Faintly green
loops confusing white
antinomy, this type

keeps certain course by
turning luff, lies off
burning coastlines,
rustling and embroiled:

be careful in restoring
such a colony –
is it hope or ancient cysts
infest the softening cortex.

8.

Much as a limpet glued with single foot slyly hops
one to another square, stakes a claim on shiny clinker
taps too for energy, gone to ground they don and doff,

out of devilment switch post, flip down to establish
foot pedestal, hence further fit stone perfuse or spool
threw in the balance feathery multicoloured flagella,

seething of sargasso weed contriving such as surely
mitigate opacity with tentacled and thin-fingered
bloody filter-ways, pump European historical arteries,

leaf this marble pavement, re-stencil the horizon of
a Lombard or Atlantic passage, silk of untamed sheen
not to be mistaken for lucidity with barbed trip-wires.

Homeless colour stains the ruined station, hot blood
with its wash has dyed those seas whose incarnadine
oval portrait apertures and dawns as reported, weep,

inculcating in the ear that keen lament whose timely
outrush carries off an eyeful or its spasms to transmit
likenesses, but the lattice, but the grading tray insists,

clamant waves lash incessantly a single foot footsore,
foot shackled in a violet pool, sunset dragging blue
bruise until the webbing galaxies conceive the mass

needful to shrink back the blood blisters tumefying –
check, not reserve a passion spatters on descendants
crawling to the rock tables shedding limbs as they go.

Behind opacity bright filaments divulge to each other,
shadows stretching past spring shut. Now electronic
tags report a break in parole, gluing them by ankle.

9.

Thick compliance has been figured like guidance tech
Colour wash in blue brine and pale pink leucocyte
misty over stacks thwarted by the pressure pad of sky

Cling here, cling here, secure the Atlantic fastnesses
Green, grey, black stain rock with arsenic and tin flush
Clear the site Long blades pulverise founding debris

abject pillagers sift still for early songs They bulldoze
towers, flatten off the footings Last night once fallen,
to anchor squirming screens were moved to fake a fit

political dance amid those screens where trademarks
live, where copyrights and pass-cards are patrolling
fossil curtilage Arctic nights Desert nights Cling here:

the gallimaufry tide sweeps ashore, a runtime pulse
converges with the waves and yields The dawn breaks
within an installation caught in its simulcast embrace,

screens waft on the air, screens tremble from a polder
scrubbed of footprints that fade out on rock, bloody
jostle spreads out through a boatless whaleless waste

choked with jellyfish whose viscera stretch narratives
contract into beating hearts and grey digestive tracts
Thus screens incorporate, they encyst, thus cnidarians

throng sea encircled by the shallow land, not a stone
untoppled. Here one had once stood, here the upright
walked and aged and worked through and englanced

longingly and drank too much Where the red tide laps
sea birds nevermore alight Take this for your personal
headset and eyeset and mindset and poke at entrails.

Chysauster in Mist

Who are we, a race, a tribe, a herd, a passing phenomenon, or a traveller still travelling in order to find out who we are, and who we shall be?

ETEL ADNAN

I.

Moor swings out, travellers are taken on its liverwort
and furze along with scrawny horseflesh, shivering
like sun on racing water

Bare-headed gulls swing on banks of cumulus, rock
now buoyant with their risen sun worship, one for
the birds struts forth

Upon his airy track one resident shines and fades,
welling from his footfall a shower of micelles

Micelles writhe on the extracted world of plenty
swept with flash floods and wracked by drought

Beneath the shrunken crust day's brilliance holds its
own, none of which avails the travellers who up sticks
and grab at orbiting rocks

Hold your horses to the circuit they were destined
for, or bear the sun upon naked shoulders swinging
out on space to be avulsed

Mere crumbs, a trail of breadcrumbs loops and re-
loops in pink dots between greenish bursts of rock
you identify as serpentine

A splotch moves and the loops reconfigure. Travellers
throw saddles on the horses left running loose and
make haste forward

2.

Hear a call for transparency, a clean desert, balance
sheet. The lit, the instantly annunciated, print to their
own biometrics

Smooth between restraint and excess a rink hovers,
pasturage or metal, perfect slick allows no hidey-hole,
no fogou

Terrorism of the abstract, terrorism of the fence,
between these straight-up proud but crouch again
between systolic pulses

Graph home coordinates across the sheet, capillaries
wreck the eyeball, bloody criss-cross obliterates the
floaters

Call to detumesce. To wipe. Leave no trail. To digitise.
To sharpen each digit. Make a breast. Call for trans-
parency

Lumpish on the smoothly transitioning display crawls
the beetle-back, paisley and opals iridesce at calibrated
clicks

What do you imagine? An affluent young girl wipes
her hard disk and glitter eye shadow, stuffs her back-
pack and sets out

Debris of high-end malls, named headquarters, cam-
phorated brothels, glows through silk, decalcomania
in leaves of gelatine

3.

Fly to the border of convictions as if shape were but
their loss of traction, a disempowered glide, to shape
up meant to thicken

Went walking in the ground plan of Chysauster,
sought to bed down the idea of dilapidation, fatten-
ing in pastel dots

What had been imagined, street after street smashed,
the electronics need you here and find you located
just like that

O you scamp! The wilderness wags its tongues, even
so where is the forming throat, where do you squat to
scoop pond tribute?

Somewhere between the ring-road and inner circle
wrecked tenements fill with bobbing gulls and oys-
tercatchers

Limpet-like amid the falling plaster, children practice
hand-stands as security services talk you through the
steps

Advance your own in smart rheology. The earpiece
flowers blood, screen not shatterproof the way for-
ward clears

Must be hefted patiently to spike the grid reference,
know your place, haul along, in a trice, a trice further

4.

Clear what the cast was to be as though a splash of
flux could confound the switching mechanism, grow
itself

Compositae block ears to hypertrophy pink growths
allow, audition flap on flap and boundless swing out
in ellipses

Break bread and further comminute its ash, flowering
pores spew genotoxic slick rolled up short in collagen
and grit

Could be treble fine hash, bluish trumpets ranked
across the hanging sky drive travellers out to meat
barns

Tufted syllables in cotton sedge, washes of percussion
breaking surface, islanded, leated and fired up

Instruct how to button back, holster in a vacuole the
hushed hearer, cap-à-pie one note sounds in, anecho-
ic bell

Trees discolour and the wrought grasses hold their
place as the loop generated opens. To be signified and
not know

The shingle street claims each nanosecond, chaining
copulas of likeness. How was it boosted – how was
morning crowbarred

5.

The twisted cord of voice, furred and frayed, is still
stapled to a damp plaster wall with its impress called
Admit One

To the resident the bell calls, call holds its note,
thrown forward on a moth-eaten fringe where fat
blooms are falling

Overlay of clear nervous and digestive tracts, trans-
parent knots are straightening, unkinking, twisting so
that one cord

One outfall, one intestine flattened as a ribbon, the
ribbon rolled until microns-thin, one dangles from a
punch-card slot

Slot into the pitch classes, water clock that seeps into
plaster. A margin thickens on the desert and eats its
fill

Gauges of extreme sensitivity measure pulse, starry
trace coating sand, sand of exploded sandstone and
limestone

Submit to be inserted in an invisible façade. A build-
ing settles amid slots, scrapes the gasping throat of a
razed building

I am my border guard. Was this a stammer, no it
was the bloom stuffed in my throat, bunch of multi-
coloured wire

6.

Accosted in its shield
        mirror,
mirror one aperture
arrows fly through
        undistracted,
thump

in covenant straw
        left to rot
behind its back,
or is a shield a mirror
        warding off
escutcheon

at oblique angle,
        set
up to its blot,
        and if peeled,
sliced up, subject to
intermittent profiling?
Stunned

antennae pull back,
        fly
rolling retina, dome
of tautly loomed
threads,
shimmering in arrow

heads dunked in tar.
    A U-turn
by one shaft
twists back against
all straying sighing weft,
torches thatch.

7.

Fire took hold, fire seized, fire shook livid compote.
Upholstery put on feeble smiles,
turning to show everything which is just its point:
When I saw everything I saw one point
        evacuating.
Springs gyrate, while in gymnastic clusters gas-jets
dance across the loaded open. Suffice it the rig
workers worrying out a tongue
saw fire dance above its lolling proclamations
        unhinged
break not prevail, but slinks between a fair bunch,
flagrant line of the strobe rose ticks.
Suffice it silversmiths I thought of stirred pots of
attar must unfold exactly as they do
        calibrate
fire upon their benches, ramekins scent floods over:
Such was a mayhap convoy, such was hope,
fire broke out, a paper fire, scrunched and mashed
ash wings that flutter from the grate
        to make a point
together like a will, like a deposition sent to future
execution were it sanded well, sand
to soak the blots I think was chuted downholstery,
I sunk into the downy pillows even worse
        acoustically,
if what is found suppressed for sure shortly spread,
what flared would be unreadable,
maybe too stable element, lean passionless script
tick-tocked across the brushed and blotless desert,
        blue shadow
ramping up the kerb at which a taxi long-awaited
pulls in never, fiery asphalt a face

rests on reinforces: sunset smelting out of snippets
new birds, closer now, as if unsparked
        bales of fire
stoked below the waterline, yet from neglect itself
turning up when no longer sought,
in a fire-trap, an iron sheath, in a condemned pile,
no part of speech is permitted,
        that is the point
insignia these burnt-off gas sheaths cannot reveal,
but involute to snag what light's going.
I lamped out of there would you believe I trailed
nice, intelligent watercolours as though blots
        stress the point
shimmer stuff impossible to get a fix on, grasses
grew beneath my feet, the fetish
trailed its feathers and wore its emeralds, speaking
words in order till one point slowly opened
        sunrise sphincter.

8.

Or heard a voice crying in the desert. Or threatened
to solidify into the word but no shadow fell for the
word to nail down

The word began to foam about its edges and its nu-
cleus to churn. Look into it, the image of a galaxy is
forming

Follow where in redshift, light gathers weight. Heavy
blur like spawn starts to multiply, condenses so that
lifelines

fold about the multiplying nuclei, are these meta-
phase, linked fires that sputter, are they rails

Hitch up against the rocks. Stand as cormorants would
stay their shelf, their saucer swinging out across licks
of fire

The seat royal of this famous isle. Empty shells the
setting sun burnishes and high sun ivories in homage
to a buried tooth

O tooth it is you we worship in your lambent setting
on the windowsill amidst stiffened horsehair brush-
es, jam-jars of chromatin

Now to press forward amidst the sand-storm of pack-
ages scrunching a giant face on the lie of the land

9.

These were our idols, all of them, our watermarks, our
lost Olympians all wispy on transparent skin

A chinagraph sketch of Lenin, a squad of dissolving
Buddhas heaped by children out of sand, a fish in
sky-writing, lugworms

Treated to what-have-you, a traffic-light diminuendo,
a rummaged heart or faint kerchief or the heart's in-
cumbent

Micelles can read each other only too much on set
lines. It is the loaf they long for not the stamp on the
wafer

Water that disconcerts. The tongues of every pine
cone lick each other and convey the wood they spring
from

Crumbs invent the loaf they sprayed out of like
wood chippings, an oasis loaf, a low-lying polder loaf,
new-risen

Skin differs here, the god is flaking with psoriasis,
pots of red salve are set out by devotees before the
snowing solar face

They rub themselves ecstatically but confined with-
in their boundaries wax shiny and abstracted. Get on
with you

10.

Mist flung over Chysauster and small detachments were glimpsed, each an earful in its household shell

A boy stands guard with a rifle while his mother squats above a cooking pot balancing on debris, steadied by a wheel rim

Dark gleams from the damp earth, glinting mica in Mesopotamian sun, extinguish these, desecrate all shrines

Harebells hang lank, the iron ground is a strongbox ribbed with lead solder, fringed with yellow foam of Lyonesse

Lie down in the ground plan, turn to the metal breast and breathe on it until the mist thickens yellowish like curd

It is sifted, it is strained, trees discolour and it falls out that way that seedcases burst into utterance

Glued to linen, bark beaten out is intricately grooved and chased, its clefts shelter travellers and pack animals

Across slate and clay tables they advance in black and white, graphite rubs away ruts, scratched slate seals shafts

II.

How things turn out, as from a waste paper basket,
a paperknife, urine-yellow ivory,
ink-stamp gryphon cracked by the surface heat: how
the cable, how a star travelled down the cable, how
        things turn out
before the bay window at the apex of a gravel drive
propped a rose quartz pyramid of heroes
dallying with goddesses, diving for a crimped
chrysanthemum, bloom plummets in a root rift
        its bibelots,
a dancer kneeling on her rosewood plinth,
a palm tree gripped between their
knees by peeping cherubs, but against chip tongues
gauffering its bark, inadequate to shield from sun as
        things turn out
playing from the eyes scattering in oval miniatures
self-immolate at once, when a recognising look
draws them from their trench wet and monstrous,
blow at surface pressure, so
        be below
light compositions, stains, fleeting cloud, ballerinas,
tangle of courtiers in a fête champêtre tousling and
tossing to-and-fro a grimace or a smile –
a mock-up bull swags enormous balls, off-screen as
        things turn out
tramps squelchy pasture. Stressed idols of the deep
detonate when hauled up: did you have a prayer?
Or will be made stand to reason, brought to light
pickings laid on flagstones, exhibited on sand trays,
        bibelots,
these are gravel in a shoe, crunching like milk teeth,
playthings of a dog that nursed me set on plumped

satin. What do they scatter to forestall?
        Things turn out.
You loathe their box. You were splintering the sides
of their box. Better downsize. Which
things were you bound to sell off or chuck?
Where is your conveyance? Which do you prefer?
        They turn out.
Velvet and with drawstrings. Listen close. At what
inaccessible depth
hard sonar beads. A bay window like a bathysphere,
        I made myself scarce,
as if an up-swell might devour the tooth crypt of sky
        and below
coins clipped from circulation,
styluses, franked papers, cancelled credit cards,
mortgage agreements, warp the underlay:
        Still they pitch up,
straggling on the slant moor, full of yearning
for a skyline, paraffin breath and urine-soaked mats,
left fugitive, stateless on the heath. The whole band
        turned out
with their few things, few clothes,
their treasures and their tatters, icons and their vital
proverbs, myths that are their caravan.
Blooms droop, wretched horses slip bridles,
stray to crop at wiry tufts, prickly stalks, they suck
        winds that blow,
suck brackish, saturated purses of sphagnum. Stray
from no path, pitching camp where heather sags,
pause in placelessness – what of those things
long-past from our hygienic place turned out?

They soon will explode,
and from the depths the bibelots will strew shards
of rosewood, rose quartz gravel, clumps of oakum
     certain to pitch up,
once more will pitch up
coin hordes, burial goods, complex metal brooches,
crocus bulbs.
          Life without.

Bodrugan's Leap

Faint First of Meanings Ever Meant

Again at St Juliot

Entreaty of underbrush
        hauls down its prize,
thrashing yellow spasm
        felt as voluntary

while the sun in fiercest gall
        sucks out airy
curls from the last lockets –
        audibly they crackle,

blazing as a whirlwind
        fans images
        then withdraws –
shakes rosaries of live heads

ratcheting through air, air
        that is thin mire
        seeming colossal
in evacuated cobalt shadows.

Lain across a noon sill
        rosebuds and stems
        coil in memory,
the meagre day recovers.

Pod, bud and blossom,
        weight of a green spat.
Gorse flaks emptiness.
        An old recruit scuffs,

tongue-tied to feeling,
    vehement in
    thoroughgoing,
brushes through the prickly

barrier with no blood spent,
    map-reads across
    charred roots
shadow has occluded,

steps through frost glitter,
    seed artillery
    spitting at full pelt,
a circlet of bright heads.

The Island of Love

Vague human masks pipe out a
sweet coverture.
The isle is swarmed over by their
            bird proxies

pillaging while seeming to
bestow the crystal wink, all such
            imitation
takes its aspect from nature.

Chisels shape a loaf of rockwool,
            chipping at a coast
song bandages.
            Tulips streaked black

jostle amidst deepest clefts –
            and to appearances flop.
Silver balls roll off a table.
Intervene now: stems

thirsting for flowers, bleep
after five seconds,
inside polythene they crisp with
            emergency hydration:

the syrup drawn off is their ichor
winks clear and metered.
            What increase,
what a good package, what joy –

once he pierces the spongy pink
economy.
Dress this table perhaps. Truss
one snipe or plover each,

divert from lip to cistern lip
until his pursed mask collapses.
                    Leaving nothing
for it but to trill, trill sort-of,

nothing for it
but to make light of
          spoliation, of its spillage
slathered on the island of love.

Ward Round

Interruption thickens most
 in those quivers
  light catches for its
sleeping fire to run to form,

test-sticks scatter in
  chromatic wheels.
Screwed-up eyes will flash
  vigilant high beam,

blasting a high expansion
  foam on her chart,
pines toss over gleams
  of scrubbed linoleum,

high seas roar. Veining the
  crocuses that spike
  beneath the clock,
red streaks feed on a throat

sounding too thick report,
  all its colours
  down pat, much as
long sleep were interrupted –

until time, until time also
  ran to form,
  smashing rainbows
of inured bindings athwart.

Self Defeated

Gum brittles into lozenges. Points
    ease fine drops,
      cannula askew, oil tips
hinges and before you know, hinges

hungry for the touch they recognise,
    wrench back.
      In my view
sunk into the cuckoo-spit of over-

much grabbed then repeated, beams
    then are bessemered
      balsamic tears,
these then slot together end to end –

but congested, ironed out by sheaths
    of fibrous vacuum
      freeze in my view,
stiffen like fingers crook to collapse.

Before a simple act the mind's cartel
    claims agency,
      stamping each brow
with a logo of self-possession, self

being held in trust elsewhere, spins
    the entire compass,
      jewel bearing
shines on a unipolar pivot, stripped.

No North hinges on this decision,
     nor does a ship
     alter course towards
the pharos circling in its own beauty.

June Bug Versus Hurricane

Evacuate the outline! How
    swell ranks so limited,
who once filled the glass in their
    sensual crush

search the unresponsive
    stretched skin, and rattle
stands of bamboo. Where was I?
    Bent into a skeleton

or flourishing a marker, or if air
    between, its thin plate
shielded inner workings,
    forfeited to glass

muted but still populous,
    one silhouette cupped
her hand as though to scoop
    tabled rain, reaction

quick and nervous, flank pang
    clock-set so to
prance, prance, a shadow-
    length awaiting scratch

shuddered, underfoot as new
    prints densified, pores
burst with vivid oils.
    A first morning gull

hieing from blue distance, skims
the lamped shore,
salience is mine, in outline,
poised to cut its divot.

Central Park

Lost receptionists
fill the alcoves,
    but accept no referrals.
Each strikes a pose of diligence

frozen and emphatic.
    This is too much. Pinch
their little decencies.
Who here acts as spokesman?

One may stoop heavy-jowled
    and swing it.
Following which,
heads turn. Necks ache

twisted so, now a message flits
like a pivotal bird does
    behind his or her
avowed front.

Who leans on the balustrade?
Who holds court meanwhile?
    Her cheek
half-stumped upon her fist,
her mental cheek smiling thus?

Through its cancellations, sky
warms every niche.
    Blank spaces,
organised to shrug off what
    demands persist,
offer the set range of reflexes.

Remote Song

On polythene the leavings of syntax
　　wipe off. Let's adjust
　　the new mask
drawn from store, screws to respond

beside a tubular bedstead, harness
　　flopping back.
　　Aerosols cough
fitfully through flat and filtered air,

across dull glazing, birdsong drips.
　　As marked,
　　insert drain;
a trickle tapped from a song-thrush

won't flush through machinic hum
　　tremor-tuned: de-
　　pending fish pout,
stooped swans strain for a leaden

chime, tear-streaked fume-rooms
　　smudge clinging
　　blinds urging clear-
cuts to unchoke down their sentence

strapped breath to wall, curriculum
　　to a far pump,
　　conjoin in sound
ticking tirelessly; and lifted in chorus

the faltering verbs spill, air scatters
    labour that a flock
    thumps at glass,
eking out such as leave, flit clumps.

Burning Water

The song of sovereignty softens
    folded-up, also tuck
corms elevate green aerials.
    Squirrels kick through their

dank drays to gather tribute.
    One could I for one
enjoy the bursts that presage what
    joy might compel –

and between, in other attributes
    disquiets lie, off-
hand, hand-in-glove, sent in
    glut to work feverish mills:

surveying all, the blent window
    squawks with
periodic birds, yellow runner
    fund shakes, can't stop.

Bring confirmation to me, does it,
    someone else's dream
covey, so whose outline
    takes the biscuit? Sharp

lay-figure or emasculating bleeds?
    Underneath, rabbits
bolt through tunnels
    while the impassioned

fields shake, het up by the
      air melting through them.
But I am focused on a window,
      tracing in its float flaws

the watermark of sovereignty,
      while distant flares
show the cane trash and
gas waste combine in their apogee.

Early Evening Programme

I had more than stuffed myself
    but there was more
orange-laced and dainty
    lay on the collagen plate.

Languidly we broke cake, pulled
    over the shallows,
cast round to fill sockets,
    and our blabbing, welling,

slopped in aural saucers,
    taken by the wrinkle
of a whirlpool, of funded rocks:
    or we might capsize,

dash ourselves and clean up,
    or only bother surface,
surface that is all smiles and
    grimaces, its button anus,

button omphalos, the seam
    keeps, seam that haunts
our party on its errant scow
    dredging nonchalantly.

Trailing all our hands we
    could use our teeth to pick
the one stitch in nine
    apt to pull the plug.

Tunnel Collapse

Green sticks to its functional, mindless
    sexual spur,
    what was toed in
lingers past a phrase's date of release,

thistledown clings to its stalk, and one
    nagging placard
    occupies the entire
space to think. So *Watch for Falling Ice*:

folds persist in green and scythes stall
    at green push-back,
    falter at the wall
of such ruthless verdancy. The beasts

dance tiptoe cramped in early growth,
    velvet nubs
    unextended
bow on heads sick with watchfulness.

Strike the bronze, it wants to resonate.
    Feed shop-worn
    anecdotes,
stir up a watch committee of instincts.

Beyond such freshets lie the sparkling
    sewage farms,
    the sub-stations
relay steady load. Under surrounding

hills, tunnels have been cut but traffic
        circulates far off.
            So sits the village
illustrious in itself. Immemorial it vets

the first fumbles, every spasm filtered,
        dark stain spreads
            from cartridges
burnt after use, creeping over pasture.

The Dripping Wall

Full of want, a wall might debar itself
    but want shakes
    the bedrock, every
brick thrills, even mortared in its sett.

Ripped flapping from its wiry hoops
    a human scrim
    shrivels and a near
copse withering belittled and denuded,

hung with webs and tatters dripping,
    shreds mist. A new
    blue-chip riser
lifts a world restructured in miniature,

red-ink morning what will it deliver?
    A method tallies
    value on the hoof –
surplices of lichen rind clabber bolts

grey, rough, but shielded: as beds of
    mist roll and unroll,
    clients cling to their
cameos, kissed by cold pressing lips.

For there is and was no mother tongue,
    what they suckle
    pokes at their lips
with adhesive, implacable coordinates.

Down I Come

I had completely stuffed my stomach,
    there was more,
      more on my plate.
When I say 'no' the voice recognition

fails and asks me to repeat myself: I
    obey with a will.
      What is step-
change or tipping point or base court;

upon its fragrant mound, more piles
    compellingly,
      recruits on a lawn,
knives strop and in short night folds.

Birdsong clenches like a fist thought,
    chaffinches,
      a wheel of knives. Full
of crampons, hooks and ball bearings,

hands on thighs and easily expansive,
    I shall be burst in on,
      blather out, switch
right to left while beating featheredge

lawn in lawn, pegging down scrolled
    advice for eaters,
      stepping through fresh-
chopped two-stroke prenatal puddles.

Facing Chesil Bank

How high should this go? Air shelves
    dip down, slant
    light buttresses,
gulls cry above the slates, put it here.

Wind heavies, waves lean into sloped
    ledges, under-
    tow of pebbles
growls shaking sprung bed and turf,

noisy shingle warps banks of filters,
    bass-traps shape
    barest meaning –
wind's mantle dragged off the ocean.

Seabed ramping up climbs to beach.
    Bullocks
    low against cliffs,
breath rubs through them, warmth

tugged and worried by intent breeze
    wafts it here, shone
    from a steadfast
single bar of pebbles, like a thought

flees the moment summoned up or
    cinnamon scent
    pools on a
summer night. Like some distraught

laugh, viridian fixed and quizzical,
    motley clothes
      or personal skit,
herself as her more fanciful version:

below combes, dour sand is fretting,
    roar of sea
      draws the far-off
traffic noise; take a moment's respite,

put it to one side, a mere scratch more
    than accidental,
      not so much a tally
as a thinly-beaten disc, scuffed faint

indentation sullen water seeps into,
    the first step
      hesitating.
To be harboured, have comfort, have

ease, lie guarded from relentlessness,
    breakwater
      ploughs, compacting
shingle bulwark: the gaps suck, piles

murmur, squeezing through cavities,
    shift counter surge,
      dispersing impact
off-shore, rip-tide radiates off baffles,

making shift so making certain. Single
        out, strip back
        laden breath,
a rank, moist, suffocating cosset; bare

your head against wind made slam as
        knuckle, hung
        in bullock gloom:
cavities sluice with new insurgence,

deadpan rock will crack an entryway
        where unashamed
        scrabble-stripped
streamers of dead warmth serve to

fathom shortfall, flitch air and drizzle
        diehard, feast
        fat on failing grass,
count famine assets frankly lucrative.

The only sun is dead set on a possible,
        endured sun.
It slaps an obdurate nameplate, shines
        on hapless digits.

Its only sky stops above the huddled
        beasts at a freshet.
Ocean floor is slabbed in claim forms,
        spells and re-states

debris gripped in the dismantler arms,
    the definition roar
grades gravel. In what cleft can I hide
    this bare shim?

How high should it go? Bare like any
    thorn or gravel
      bloodying my shoe,
yanked will be harassed by noisy light,

splitting rock; or will it spring the steel
    plate from its guard,
      open present time
to the vista of expansive dying foam?

A solitary aslant shies away from vast
    waves, skirts
      edge of rockfall,
shim put here, shim considered, shim

loved past reason, shim if data-tracked
    expatiates,
      breath released
from bullocks huddling and indifferent,

shim that scribbles through exhausted
    rills of sand –
      until erased, scrubbed
at the outfall by a boom drawn across,

all havoc stilled and misery at face-off,
       tide tamps within
       hearing, in my
gulping ventricles, tide hauling back,

dragging stones into my head, thus I
       hummed accordantly.
       Where shall I go,
placeholder whose slant scrawl snares.

So Far and No Further

Burst on a rubbish dump like her bag
    hooked by receptors
    disavow the legacy of
rise and fall, all position falls vacant,

dull the stones and too meticulously
    combed for any trace
    smeared or purulent,
mites scurrying over lichen shroud.

Fog horn blurts, their misadventures
    thud into eyelets.
    Never had gaps, pores
wanted so, inviting fleas to a stretch

spring the murky eye so spray curls
    back into its blister,
    spits pewter spiders
shovel-primed as though for seeding,

strews loose rough-cuts that congeal
    on the flux floor,
    stiffening, unbudgeable.
Boulders once glistened with her look.

Devoran

Intermittently a bulge of grey
    felt would pig on itself,
even as the outer world,
    recoiling, threw out feelers,

slovening in tears of grease,
    swollen became runnels:
once apparelled in the salt
    lockdown, stood vulnerable.

There between laurel flitches
    stalked a quarryman
flourishing his mattock.
    Ever afterwards, as beasts

huddle injured and famished,
    who couldn't bear to be
confined, pick at clouts,
    opting for their captivity.

Dressing-Up Box

Void but even there a spark plays.
    Just try: a log I dragged
through the doldrums
    couldn't gauge its scope.

Then saw such exchanges meted
    out, knots slacken,
lines begin to fray in this harness,
    varnish flake as night

thrown its foregoing crust.
    Then saw the lake dwellers
pack boats idling alongside.
    Cloud put on bulk,

consommé dripped from clouds,
    while at a window-seat
picked apart flesh tassels,
    gold, carmine tips to lash,

tethered should they happen
    to inch outward. As
when one deep-dragged hawser
    flopped, as when I yawed,

veins I carburettor, veins I muffle,
    veins I be singled out
for the spark you induce,
    leaping between poles.

Unclassified Road or Track

See how this avenue once led me on
    in inglorious laurel,
     collapses like a lake
destined to bear anything, thwarting

neither rain stroke nor drizzle, floats
    spawn and chrysalis,
     nub or drifting nymph
embarking on its green passage, kin

sorely feel the need of. Shall I batten
    off you now my links
     fail to fetch? Strands
of pure now in parallel! A menacing

tree-feller smirks, flicks his thumbs-
    up. Get on with it,
     smite the laurels,
strip them of their thick glum foliage,

hostile projections that had loitered
    this side of sponge
     windows, sliding
into cloud heaped like roadstone grit.

Open the lockers, let the path ripple.
    Damp trees raise
     awnings for a follower
sepulchred in cloud, given air burial.

Base Camp

Defiantly familiar notes strike home.
    A squalling upon grass
      yet more audible,
places volunteers for Those Steeps.

From time to time upon the saddle
    glancing nervously,
      recruits set on a path
stall, so even with your flying leg,

amputated wheel and baked goods,
    every next step
      slips on rubble. Soft
undulation, jaw-jaw, tuned purée,

conspire to hamper progress, seal
    within a long pipe,
      liable to dragoon back –
so if pain flares as here and now it

does as shown in lights on a panel,
    and if only one
      emotion were
felt instead of present and correct,

if the architecture of such feeling
    would stabilise,
      eyes and muscle
gel, would Those Steeps not submit?

Time chews the poor conscript out,
    tents pegged on
    fat slopes,
vacate when reveille dies at dawn.

The mournful notes won't ever fade,
    gashed like pellets
    of grey tea, hot
water strikes, blousing into jellyfish,

skirl and spin after an effort, crows
    slip like loose scree,
    flash across every
quartered flag, be it spread or furled.

Expected News

A platform lowers and the sun
    traipses across the yard.
Mighty sup at the trough,
    such a turn-up, such soil-furl,

lie down and roll over; eyes
    sleeve a threshold
serpentine in paperclip
    ridges where the day-to-day

would rotely lie spaced out.
    Paving stone sensors
like as not, would like as not
    ping, were they not settling

dumbfounded. I feel partial.
    Track me by my broken stick.
Soon the entail will abolish
    even traces of shadow.

The Systematic Beds

Is that the stuff we wanted to
        feel firm beneath our feet,
or set in village dry-
        cleaner's cheery greeting?

Telepathy had churned it over,
        bone splinters poked amid
blotch at the tumulus, a
        thumbprint, a soak-away

sank under each logged name...
        Did this one correspond
to her actual wilfulness?
        We leant on instruments

since any reading would work.
        Trapped in that quagmire
all the same we re-emerged,
        weltering towards a copse.

There guns and mantraps
        stroked each's face's edge,
only now seen reflected
        in a striped dog-bone haft

cutting you and me both from mud-
        thick embankments,
for was that fissure long-sought
        chisel script amulet.

Compelling where biology
    disserves, creaking
sky does its most emphatic job of
    arms crushed round us.

The Cloches

Don't tamper with the packet. Check
    tare weight. Free
animals from the idea of freedom,
    bang a cedar chest shut.

All their cavalcade squeaked in
    button answers,
night shouts and rhythmic silence
    loosening the tiles.

They marched on knotted paths –
    at intersections, liable
to collide, leant into zigzags,
    broke corners off even so,

pink stuffing marmoset or
    lobster packed into its sleek
pneumatic tube,
    got sent for re-stitching –

animals traipse through my head
    banging on the pillow,
the anaesthetic
    sheath of tingling cement.

Up Jenkins. See you mine.
    She squats between rows
balancing a trug, now watch her dig,
    watch her heft, trench,

raking over, now bend,
    offering her implements,
able to restore their beasts
    into their snug benefice.

Behaviour of Starlings

Fear tilts, as seven squalling neighbours
      rush to crease an air corridor;
joy does likewise, such innocence
      funnels and distends, a trap,

a lobster pot of sorts below. Wanderers
      knit its interwork – a space
occupied binds the flightpaths tighter:
      change of state, insurrection,

crystal cake that's yanked from solution –
      old régime or new arrays freeze.
Look where high myriads sheathe
      volutory from feared swoop:

sky bears no scars, all particles regroup.
      A straggler pinned to earth
in ash or snow, satellite-identified,
      his path too can entrench hope.

Wapping Steps

Once had it been transparent
    Once vetted
Snagged as though on purpose –
    purpose catches

Once had blackberries ripened
    Once fingers
dabbled in horological oil –
    not incidentally

Once your mouth on wet steps
    Once if furze
glitches once if stars burn
    steel and catch acid

Once did unsheathed pits well
    Once new swarm
stood on ceremony
    over what once sunk

Once laid out the crust belied,
    once tar sands
crust on a riper purple melt,
    blood my sweet

Once it was as it might be
    in succession,
much still might have
    snagged here to purpose.

Second Building

Slam into the gravel curve,
    tumble on a pleached
slope, crossing shadow
    to its throne, plunge

where shadows mass,
    where future tenebrism
treacles, stumped they may be
    but yet thicken:

chiselled into blocks
    construct this temple
to self-presence, stopped
    in a cupola. Such is

how spendthrift lovers,
    twinning mouths,
parting lips about horn,
    lips against a stigma's

coral tongue, lick a lily's
    anther or a rhizome
sharp as jet, light a thorn-
    tree of wicks, scraping

branches cleave the dome:
    This is once for all.
This is just the once
    shines in its flowering.

What temporises still,
        squamous in shadow?
What draws its path
        behind, on the springy

rough? Throws a voice above
        purple pools?
Will not ever cease
        knitting and unknitting?

Out of the Blue

No not so devoted, what shortly followed
    nailed the canard –
    a CCTV trained
on their composure set them by the ears,

contorted like a whelk a turret topped all
    monstrously,
    flew the flag
above an IED tucked in, don't dare jog it,

pram rocked in after-blast as foreordained
    burst the drum
    set out for this,
capped propane, roof capped with shells.

Leaf-springs quiver, hiss of stop plummet
    sharpens what
    to hear, reveals
what a floor was: explosion floods in light

bedroom walls, the bedroom now a gallery
    swings apart,
    exhibiting the pair
in love-making more detached and frantic

writhing over punched plaster, map tables,
    writhing over deep
    flock decor,
blistered hot below their stripped exertions.

What echoes still on the landing, unboxed
        stairs? Disabused
        empty cry,
cry of stymied love, sounding retribution,

love corrupted in its doll's house, so long
        soothed and smothered,
        works both over –
and pink noise and debris stiffen their ears.

Café Terminus

for *Steve Tifft and Anita Sokolsky*

Do not drop the carry. As vaulting sea
    fidgeting at high cliffs,
     quarrying the
buttresses, propelling billows' salt hit,

tense if no lineaments a glass blistered:
    Lay the fuse,
     set the timed
bulge or chancre hardening by friction

being the furthest rising to their timely
    call for time,
     runs up against
second hands rehearsing the composed

percussion caps: Trace the fuse's path.
    No plotting, no
     prequel follows,
veils descend from jurisdiction a future

violence will impersonate, haloed by its
    history as though
     a Brocken spectre,
pure deed held in a gash of iridescence,

walking on the water glassy in its calm.
    Cupping glasses
     hang from a
horizon's bar in readiness to bleed hard.

Again at St Gorran

Who shivers in pyjamas and his vest, nil to
        investi-
        gate, what's
to see, introspect, focus on his mark sheet,

as if a stubborn child hustled fast off-ramp,
        dropped on
        rubber studs,
child screaming Shit! in front of hen coops,

detailed in the small hours for hosing shit,
        morning clanks
        obedient pail,
walks his ramp to where his swollen goats

butt the stalls, where at an upraised switch
        hot piss fills
        his dungarees:
I'll undress myself, I'll dress myself down,

I'll take care of it. Over white cotton files
        spreads a rash,
        stinging rash
nipples every inch of ramp pissy evidence.

Pause a while to hear the ocean surge, tree
        tops sway,
        nestle each
against the waves lapping in a haven, safe

for hard-wired and upstanding caregivers,
    until he stands
    before the pump,
scrubbing at his stains and being dropped:

processed at a bay tribunal, shit meted out.

Lonely Women

The curve that ends but will not close in that cedilla hung
Rough-cut umbilical and that's that except that swings
What but an abstract heart compels, heart unrequited drop
Open as the prospect skies the conifers, cloth hoses snake
Supposedly a hydrant hills in brushstrokes slightly wetted
Finds a deal and chipboard house damp, echoically bereft

Ends to be subscribed link their soft connectors and close
They can't allow exceptions that contaminate the spray
What should it be requited, tongues are lolling postulates
Stricken violins were forthright, cloth I had been cut from
A woman wets with her tongue and pivots brushstrokes
Overseas conifers are crowding light out from her house

Subscribe to this or not it ends dangling like that curlicue
Swinging over emptiness figuring as unity's apotheosis
Say 'we' into its streaming gash lest requital seal its flap
Descending in a fine spray and braided snakes of quench
A disassembled cube that opens upward to a view of hills
Beneath a falling dusk a muffle, sodden traffic so bereft

Such are the cedillas swinging on her earlobes in the dark
Umbilical that broken once a mother leaves unidentified
Abstract love completes the monumental sea and surges
Round its shoreline the collapsed lie like stricken streams
Even so above the hills a blue vapour now imbues, it must
A child rattles chipboard walls enraged and snaps his cue

Run Sheet

Here: scraps demanding an expert response
    tumble from between
    sheets after a decade –
receipts, hard satsuma peel. In case of blood

breaking surface, bruising shadow into flesh,
    restitution falters.
    Could blood flow back
again to blue the edges neglect had injured?

Here: heaped liquorice wheels, a thick-tread
    barrage off-shore
    Here: the tracks
escorted by gulls' cries and penitential sirens

extend the length of hard-ridden vertebrae,
    promulgate a cause-
    way line the multi-
purpose vehicles progress along: sense their

shadows rippling round the scrubbed ridges,
    fill in their blanks,
    dreading that the
loss will be palpable, grab at any stick, grasp

fistfuls of fine sand water's suckers crumble,
    shredded ghosts
    of the adult flick-
houses prickling with nostrils' reminiscence,

dead margins the blood won't animate. Here:
   do your worst with
    junked scraps,
chew down, drag a nail then sniff their esters.

The Law

Left stateless and denied support,
    left to float as-is
pending verdict handed down, self
    self-consumes

even when remanded into custody,
    appearances conspire
against its organs, silent
    self minded to plead.

Scrub that. As-I-was had wriggled
    from its bassinet,
as-I-then-was wriggled next
    from this heap it pupped

squirming on a mud mattress,
    law of the instincts, say.
The reconstruction of both
    narrative and focal points

moves sideways over mudflats,
    wriggles from an old cast,
to be ingested, spat out,
    caught in its very act,

to be extruded, harvested,
    debride the outer show,
perhaps the worst of it, the least
    a caddis-worm, say.

Nonetheless, nonetheless, bladder,
     kidney, left to float,
bleeding on a monstrous floor,
     born from self spasm —

each rings true within a spectrum;
     the functional organs
co-operate as one, buzz on one
     execrable frequency.

Bodrugan's Leap

Where vacancy overcomes these ruses of
    navigation, arrows
      of a plotted course,
vessels more than once stuck in rockwool,

they react in strip alignment, indiscernibly
    they merge, a runaway
      must dodge their
mise-en-scène, in disguise attain a clifftop –

jump from broken turf to where a dinghy
    writhes on shoulders
      of a deep-dyed
but trustworthy sea, a boat that shudders,

tense for his plunging onto its thin planks –
    He locks oars,
      confident the course
is his to set, that it is his to forge forward.

Cotton tufts proliferate above a sheer drop.
    A white rash
      creeps upon an empty
map which no individual trace will mark;

another ruse, a few spars had drifted off to
    leeward to disappear,
      where vapour
covers cold sea and rolls onto ghost rocks.

That cannot be the story. Flowers shake
   along the brink, wild
   garlic further back
is tonguing, the pooled air is steeped in it.

The Immaterials

Arrested by the nameless, former
    names lose their hold,
    can respond
only to their echoes, shaken loose

from rock fissures creased
    deeply with the
foregoing, more definitely named.
    Can I see credentials

lost or disposed of did you say,
    father took
    his due turn, stately
in the hill's lea, took calls blocked

by sand in its turbulence.
    Mother in her turn sank,
    hushing
cries like a baffle: got beaten back

by newcomers jostling forward,
    eager with
their carborundum voices,
urchin shell that crackles

seamed in red about a nameless
    cluster of the
    pink, shining
progeny: buck up like a botched

family chorus, filling in
    for one another,
writhing, moaning up on bleak off-
shore platforms thick with guano.

Schlummert Ein

Eyelids, fall softly, from their gritted corners
    chalk, let it drizzle,
      let the streams flow
thick with a waste glaze, let imagery run off

its surplus of kaolin, choke feed of sediment
    plumed into the blue,
      tulipping its stem.
Cress bunches thickening in shallows, flukes

stinging flank heifers in their shove and jostle
    down a bank, drinking,
      mud caking lips.
Eyelids, fall softly, let me linger interrupted

behind the curtains billowing with images,
    how the unseeable
      sill even so snags, how
the very point lights from behind, thoughts

dispersing into folds slung aloft in sea mist,
    impermissible point
      breaks every motive
falling back behind the eyelids that then fall.

I breathe, I look, I carry forward, I can sense
    the last of you, taking
      walks of air thick with
waste breath your form displaces. O curtain!

O rail! I hate the thick floor beneath, breathe
    over a market quarrel,
     rise over the bass
sawing at its stems to crash down the vault,

let the vault branch recklessly, light-streams
    maze, air's stirring
     carry song back and forth;
I hear your recorder pipe, long for its repeats

giving what-for to earth seeming to attenuate,
    rock is marked
     with your aeolian flow.
Eyelids, fall softly, the cast of their fluttering

fans across the inlet a white shadow, writes
    over deep-set floor
     captivated ripples.
World, gaze out! Rise from a shrouded point.

In Memory of Sara Wilkinson and for Liz Miles

Birth Spasms

To th' trunk again, and shut the spring of it.

Entablature of Mud

The towpath where all labour is over,
    lost souls wandering the banks
shoulder their ropes in loops.
    These are the promises they hold
as though life depended on them
But the pollarded trees refuse,
signposts reduce to mere words:
    Should a deep draft canal carry
        goods to the mouth,
cracked baked mud where larvae feed
on shrinking pools
    holds pain tongue-tied in truth.

Celandine

If here when once arrived succumbed,
being looked into, had here once broken out in
blotches,
were here the stretched apparel, a patch pocket,
were a heart fomented with earwigs and lice
    Though cupped
      in one hearthstone socket
        /ball and joint/
might it multiply and become over-detailed –
          Biscuit glaze.
Finger skin-flake twirl.
Posed in gingham
    slantwise at the rock, slantwise
at the slate chimney-breast
      Then a cramped nest broke
its doll and the doll needs, must be broken,
viewed in its plurality. Smashed into heat.

Best not look too closely, get too close.
I know I have this yellow streak decomposes
    even as it settles loot best,
screaming blue murder when grass underfoot
springs resistant to Atlantic grief mutter
    gives way
        . What need to scramble out.
You patently adore sun and your eyeballs
bear looking into, as a fierce host.
       A doll once it shows up
recedes.

I bleach the spot I look at
and the spot looking back wears me out
splintering a china cheek in sodden grass –

no escaping the heat of such scrutiny.
That identifies an ant badge
I sport like an after-image
pilfers the retina for what it disperses scuttling.

Thrift

Wrest tip of valve clear away from that clinch
squeezing on it,
    laconically sprays
uncontained by what lies embedded,
      scaly creature.
Eyes welt the brink, cross-
match applies its mortar, disavows
parts seeming to match in say tufts of rubber
      creaturely bundles out.
        Moist
ground would be my habitat, crept north
in carbon tentacles. Oiled
baking tray Can you fetch that over for me
    . Scour the platen with white spirit
soon to evaporate.

Thick pasture play-pen
sloped as my defence shield before a precipice.
Sheep, gulls, high moorland kept in check
    .reinforced granite shield.
A squared-off tongue pumped up
      acid swill,
I fought to pull my tongue free Had almost
dashed on the rocks
    Watercress, thrift,
Jacob sheep toe-to-toe
charged onward to the very brink,
    cropped into Atlantic
folds cradle Lyonesse.
Could I be held? the waters are still booming

through their blowhole.
      Creatures garbed in sleep's entirety.
Could one another be out of the oceanic flock
bundled.

Touch on all fours checks valves, waves hunch.
What grabs me will discard me forth.
      I wish to feel attachments and to
love them perseveringly.
Over grass the unsorted parts are straggling
      Gather, take stock of these,
now despatch.
Doll yourself with scales of a full body armour,
      tumbling out.

Sea Aster

Restorative that picture was previewed
    I had no sense of a picture
Then the sound came back
    Could I know there had been sound?

Blue metal bloom
took the white by storm
    one inch more towards the well
An inch more
    balancing the
shining blemish
On her head as though an actor
    Rose and descended
in its flap. Metal nipple.

Restored the picture shows a harpsichord.
Venous stock distrait.
    There are links
hand point vault beach. Every ringtone dove
does touch
    . slaughter, confederacy.
First let me deal with the dog.
Cedar press disgorges my lost clothes.
Forthright swan hisses.
    Runs of ivory
foam above iron treadles mostly knew.
    Blood fails her cheeks'
blue permeating.
On her head as though an actor drains off.

The picture was restored
    I had no clue how a picture
with its sound came back
    How there was sound
except through a rip
sound flooded into. It skirls.
The flap bangs. The first-born caws.

Blindsided

Caught sight of it though overcast, pressed to
parry though forward, knowing it would swish
its twin silver trace on an unadopted bridleway,

mapping pipework scuds beneath the retina,
blood supply, crawl space, hypodermic, since
a vein might collapse, taking sight as prevision,

sight unseen scurrying on wet scree, pressure
points not clamped forthrightly must be let go...

The hum tone switches to extractor
I was standing there in the instant pot roasts
        offering my shot of what-have-you,
        cut-&-dried, fast-chilled
Something like that but not that quite...
Blinked eventually what else do I have to trust...

What I had been meant for
What once might have occupied this space
            Now stone stoppers
lately smashed between my teeth, knuckled
        hands in evidence – I took pains to suck –
O scram! to the ill-lit, stirless glade:
        Mab,
will-o'-the-wisp, lead!
            o'er the quag's dire details,
lead this spectre, giddy-up!
            I spit and spew its pabulum,
            I spurt vitreous medium

boiling in the cast in my eye,
    spatter on cramped walls the
incandescent flux bar filaments streak over,
    counter-signed, endorsed,
snapped to front as the warp of the soon-to-be:

Cross-caught scrawling whom I eyed lacklustre
    I was the pits. Sure
I was something else. Fell behind. Was sent
away.
        Beyond the giddy limit.
Feared the bleeding edge and the green point.
Pedigree ripped from my stall.
Vacancy off-paper, off-course, off the books.
            Tiptoe
courtyard, stone clapper, they too shift beneath,
nuancing to ear and eye where I might pace
lengthening,
    hissing of lost attributes, lost heritage
        soft-brushing, labelled mine...

For I shall recognise myself in the cloud mosaic,
I am a human sketched in the dewfall tracery,
whose piping might show through at any
            awkward moment

    Saving such discovery,
if cleaving to my raiment not its trail of damage,
cloaked but forgetful, hurt by its reticence,
I pieced my tracks...

pieced my pettifogging course…
    the cast of my ordinal cast...

Ranks of interferers smashed the tooth lantern
Such externals, such embellishment...
      Scoured ground was staring
hatefully, broke cover, broke
through screening voice-patter, leaves' screen...
The ground was surging
    out from its testable, its manifest
even-keeled,
    lustrous, revealing ground, ground
of the ground deeply embedded liable to gape.

Will more information enter through that hole?
Through the tear in the retina?
Judge. Challenge. Attend. Weigh. Respond.

Across the retina regardless colour branches.
Omniscan wets cotton pads, eyeballs yet lithify,
and I out of these cracks breed as do insects.

Pinks

A cry in the ice cavern leapt like a tracer shot.
Skirmish at the mouth in languages outcast,
    later in
    combative reason
forced me back
locked in brightness, locked in ice
servers. At birth memories were added.
Broken out I stumbled towards warmth before.
I thought I was my intimate, another's
unadopted language
jabbers split from the side which I had left
        scatheless, mine,
would that more than fleeting others' access-
codes in their cubes melted
out in the day.
But this was no case of one or the other.
    You had found yourself pressed –
and by you I mean you, you!
onto the earth and were my cast of feeling,
nervously into the crumbling still-warm soil,
terracotta warm with gone bodies,
    lent me what
I have to get along with, tagged
    appliances of wrenched child pieces,
casts I might model after and into
    out in the day
beside.

Scallop the dependable curtain of tar.
Crunch into material with pinking shears.
Hand me that tape.

There will be no more excursions.
     Forthwith on birth
     salt side
flanks me glittering and walls weep
ineffectual bonds and sealants, granite's
own weight staying walls from collapse.
Whitewash glows phosphorescent.
Still before the shocked hearth materials pass,
and monstrous within weeping walls
     a floppy anvil
sprouts like an ear. Its underlife
supports a slate patio. An image ghosts into life
in your bath. Your button
kept my other genitals from falling out.
Nothing ever leaks from this open mouth
     shielded in the shining ice globe
all the day we shall know
hovers above.

Magenta

Every single one of the rest had been violated.
We pressed ourselves against hide,
we pressed ourselves onto a yak wool throw.
        I saw my ice capsule
float in the drained blue way above
and there was nothing for it.
Outside gravel chippings being swept
along a gouged track,
            tar for subsumption
                    moiled in boilers
curtained in tar,
                    overflowed,
outside overflowed, hardening at the fringes
        yellow sky seeped into, canopied
and hardened.
        All or nothing, that was the sum,
steps faltered even though
        isolated stars signal to be tacked up –
though underpinned by webs of
projections, as you were,
        fall back, that's your lot, surely is.
O split stopper always were my fallback,
        all or nothing,
O split blind trunk fall back,
only to be cancelled or electromagnetic
pulse corrugating time dismantles sunders
pulse. *Noli me tangere.*
Just remove that mark
        in a twinkling/ in a flash/
fields of power will be unconscionable
        shrivelled tremor.

Every syllable has been marked
    one and by one/
seeded with a confident up-yours
    despotic idiom spills over.
Fall back to blockage.
Beyond the tufted field meteorites shower.
On the field rabbit shit.
Inside our tent air thickens now we huddle.
    Our escape capsules long departed.
Geospatial analysts have their fix on us.

Alizarin

The breathing pillow is rolled out
Birdsong is scattering its first sharp notes

Thick birdsong carpets the orchard
Curls of cold night air stir rags of blossom

Went cast forth into diversions of our own
Forging our way for no way lay before

Through immense foggy banks, roll on roll
of barbed fog, spikes of juniper, sharp

erect fins, tongue-lashings, measly
and obscure stars rashing inconsistent folds.

A dawning in pink tinge was despondent
Not dawn as dreamt towards but low-slung

Singing for our bated breath, dangled
off sticking points, pinned on nothing much

In response when boughs lash out at dawn
shrugged off gnarly-barked apple orchards

Carded tufts of mist dragged in moss
Here lay aspects. These have to be touched

have to be imagined hard. What is walked
on, sailed above, stung into the surfaces

made actual and innervated, paths
to walk across in a state of helmsman calm

beside one we have to murder, pack down
Dredgers strip clean the sea floor and the

heights once scaled were fire-raked
Seams plough the air, need that underpins

puckers shipping lanes, thickens foam
Tracks metalled, splotches hang as apples

Licits in rotation scald. As solder spots
at first frost their death becomes permissible

Time turns to gravity, grinding to a halt
A red gold runway gleams on a frozen lake

Seven suns balance in the realm of animals
Seven suns balance in the realm of ghosts

High air burns while gravity releases song
Song clattering upon ice like arrows.

World of Sentient Beings

In rising their spread adjusts.
    Might you have felt angelic,
flesh creature, scrounging round the scrap
    accoutrements, the earth-
bound vehicles whose entry failed –
            but fain
    to rise angelically
unknown to itself goes on to importune,
          revealing
only spread without limit,
    only universal fledge. Revolving
far beyond the tally,
keep your eye fixed – revoking,
    watch the flea launch, re-enter,
unscrutinised the irritating earth
    opalises, pearlises,
        swathes itself in glorious negligence.

Cease fretting at why being here nor there:
    the pimpiest, the leather-
girt outrider, chevron of slew red,
    ellipse of skeins
strung with ironical greetings cards'
    all-too-obvious poke,
    these cut through fluffed-out
curtained, moiré or glaucous light,
caramelise the ripple, mess the overlap,
    candying a would-be
nub, the nut-hard carapace that springs off
    flea-exact
or exactly brinks. Jump to that.

A swan's wing might break your arm.
A flock of angels might smash city-dwellers
into their component mouth-dams or casts
or thimbles or braces –
　　　shards that forget their forms
through shivering ecstatically.

Various are the longed-for breaks
and swarming with their intellectual
residents, leaning to insinuate
the same animal smarts, clumping to scrape
incautious hands with mineral
bait-&-switch,
　　　the fury of the fossils
visible only through the galvanism
rising between cheeks like working mouths,
set in foreheads like loggias open to
collapsed plumes,
acceding through the bone with feelers
scratching at the tympanum,
feathers pelt down as transfixing arrows.
　　　Faces angle up,
　　　clouds crawl over them
and they are made general, made boilerplate.
Angels form
into clouds, clouds into shelves. The fog-
horn booms and shakes to the surface

naked, ravenous and violent
　　　scrunched hard babies.

Sea Holly

Like a bruise a released smile mauves and
    self-devours,
while opening its punctured counterpart
    some allow to sing through.
From what has been left visible,
    a spade perhaps, a darning-egg,
the night is mitred and the corrected
    profile broods in fierce repose
betwixt a scratchy bough and spatter
    settlement – time-limited
cluster over which a weather front installs,
    much as one fleeting smile
might daisy-chain:
                 hands fold on shadow-
    rafts trusted and seaworthy,
stack a breezeblock home in an adjacency.

Distance turns along the spline curve,
    this I want I don't want for my due:
This I want bestowed, such beauty
    Where are the brindled slow-release?
Stationary limbs fill with weight
    Now lift them. Do the heavy lifting.

Clouds echo, is that consciousness?
    Steam knots, is I in apposition?
The humming block leavens far and wide
    like groundsel blooms on
property lines, from agitated thresholds,
    wind-blown seeds disperse
yellowing hill and watershed, flax

absorbent paper sops excess,
and ocean yellows also, even though
a humming fattens unbreached.
Pipe me to pastures still and parallel,
rock lizard of that custody
was ever headland raised aloft as half-
coherent coast, falls to landfall, *all*
twists buoyantly beside
I have to say it lifts.

Hinges

for Jessica Stockholder

Wings that will alleviate
keys bunched under a gloss black coping,
wings that willing long-haul grace
    slide their ailerons of red
blue and purple,
sails for a suppose-earth, a speculation
    apt to be defunded and wound up –
wings whose metal flaps on curved space,
    shake off their clips, billowing –

being how the door panels gleam at night
    in their strip,
being how they gull-wing
earth's vehicle, wobble and then flap
    compost undercarriage/
carcass that elects
    metal harp for its official
    nest of drawers
light settles in, the fund of shrimp, a fund
of cracking ice,
still a modular steel tube
    blows the hoopla feathers up –

Suppose the yellow, and black, and pale,
    and hectic red – suppose

colour strip that shoots its rising thermal,
    floats its dazzle-
strip and half-moon and wing,
        over the compounding
force trained on a transient

      scuttled by a pontoon,
military road, this or that
        blockaded shore –
a supposition-causeway –

Wings that will alleviate
compacted in their season,
        uncleave, ribbon
barcaroles encrypted in the clay/
plum blossom scrolls shrunk into nodules,
      bound to shake open.
Wings that sweep vermilion curves!
Yearned-for that behind ruffle
muslin from an engine block!
      The gangway has been folded,
      belts snag.
Spinnakers of mud music!
Sheets catching their accordant breeze!

Suppose sheets were washed and pressed
as though guests might call.
      Air miles still plummet in their
ice chunks,
fume from nimbostratus pits.
Tenenda get ripped off jagged peaks.
Above the fledgling city, clauses clack,
      a harp of steel
tenses and rushes its glissandi
sweeping down as though a monoplane
hurled at a landing strip and loading bay
      blew hectic feathers,
      wings fixed,
plunging down space in its surfacing.

Everything must fall together.

Fugitive Sheets

Stone Aperture

Blood dries to sealing wax.
Interred in its entry her head
lantern within a wall,
shone against its grating,

multiplied on bloody disks
behind the wall's calendar.
After nine an aperture
flowers as to gulp sky,

decoupled heads retort
fire at the appraising
sunlight, sheet shook below,
picked-out bits a kit for

flat truth, for innerness,
replicating one by lips,
ingathered eye, the nipple
trim-marks nudge to true,

true within the precincts,
cinctured in that stain where
beholding yet flowers.
True register will show

the immaculate, the thought,
the idea, the blueprint,
eye's brittle seal
stamped on a rush of parts,

it stirs the blood, bakes
the bloody eyepatch of unity,
aligns to a yellow spot
engulfed in a sun-infused

courtyard whose guild signs
light will bleach by way of
slurry from its macula
flooding into hollows,

stressing a contracting,
dilating point of view: what
takes a fix will blow out
lines in fluted columns:

no unfolding, no becoming,
the bars between which
melts a lesser light,
ripple round one fearsome

singularity: stark profile
in the ranked facade
multiplies, sun oversees,
thrusting back in alcoves,

constricts what might have
flowered, in the melt
of signets setting hard,
each warded by its shutters.

Liquidation

Earlier in the waniand I woke.
The statues had been liquidated,
ground up milk of magnesia
fed to the vanguard for their bones.

Seat to seat, naked metal curves,
those squirming deniers
had been rationalised, pumped
in cavity walls of an arts mall.

Courtesy of a phantom circuit
temptresses were blanked,
poured in childproof tubs on the
long night's production line.

Let me know how many. Thirteen
in a hot tent claiming land,
mothers soon conveyed in an
incomprehensible dialect,

keep this notice for future use,
a lone plastic splint, the
peristyle of concrete smashed,
fed back to its schema. The beach

smooths out your debris:
who scale the morning mist
and bathe in liquidity, towelling off
where swelling seas culminate.

Airstrip Returned to Grass

Beneath the sway, what-
ever rises to succumb,
recreates a prairie
seeded with wild grasses.

About the terraced yard,
ponies forced with spikes
into a ring of freedom,
bite from silken halters.

Canvas and cable skirt
the trackside, irrigate
pumped libraries
inventive men will access

using flashy hand-helds;
next year shows results
wrapped already,
frost certain to unearth

some decorated tile
a wrecked kiln had fired.
It needs a history,
a caption that provokes:

Can it be so inscribed,
slabbing volume?
written on a false tomb,
balks the unforthcoming?

Well?
Put your hands away.

Sway stalls on the prairie.
Swell groans in a grating.
Horses circle. Hoops
to crawl back through.

Meigs Field

Small planes once found their bearings
dropped beyond the towers,
hoisting up for subliminal meetings
eyes that follow silver hints and roll out,
swollen into vagueness.
     A glider for a portent
trawled across sunset.
A set of points that once connected,
even had been thought through as a swarm,
     dissipated,
days of two-stroke and dandelions.

Turn in this direction. The scratching
persists but that is no good answer,
nor does the horizon
self-distinguish to release the planes,
     to scatter silver pins
beyond the mind's capacity,
signalling an angelus of mannikins.
The sky stays clear as muck and
every reading fades immediately it's taken:
     falsity
twirls needles in this dense shimmer –

falsity puffs hard at stacks of glitter,
there is no fire without contrarious smoke,
nor sparks without obliteration,
     foil to show against.

Fix bearings, climb the murky stair,
burning blowflies,
pulling spider legs and wrenching
dogleg turns. Drawn by the reflector's echo,
plot a path immune to anxiety,
        right as rain
hissing on hitherto soundless figments.

Fuchsine

for *Andrea Brady*

As though the overcast might tweak
    an airman's maps, his foretelling –
as though in chains of stop-start
ischaemia, I count myself unstressed,
I walked along the human promontory
rough-tongued as sugar paper,
walked from the metal-bashers' shop,
    vinegar and cayenne
sprinkled, spiked my glass of milk.
        Well-set icing blistered.
        Ice set into cats-eyes.
I walked through the empty lot
    the enormous empty lot
towards the store beckoning me, soon I
    turned my back
on every now forgotten unit. Get yours
I said. Get yours.
And I kept mine in ghost capital.

Such was our material ease that year in
plenteousness, in full flush.
Sumptuous but interfusing, basking
    all the while June
was leaching sweetly,
        bite like molasses.
The block the far side of the apron
squatted with capacity.
Happy to take things as seen
    I browsed, I window-sloped,
honey lanyards brushed my lips.

Then I too was stopped by the incident,
     the episode, the voice that spake,
     lushness hit the doldrums.
Frigate birds collapsed on ice,
     wings like stick pyramids.
I stood dangling my bunch of keys.
Saw in the lake's heaped frozen
     waves a new car
exhibition, restaurant, luxury housing.

This then was the block whose feed I
     hung upon,
suckling on the live stream so generous
I could overflow,
creeping to within earshot,
stealthily advancing within reach,
     this then was the source
     marooned in transitivity,
flushed pink where sky spins and grips
or tries but soaked it slithers off,
its dazzle-shroud sagged
     sopping with new storylines,
slid down in folds, pleats, bales of
episodes.
               Lines aspired to mottoes,
mottoes to a motionlessness
tethered to reflections on void lagoons
where intermittent light spelt FAR LESS:
Blemished forms of love

Loving fault must needs be filled
        But the field is made of faltering,
we walk on thin ice,
images that relay genital parts.
Look, each of us knows
what we could do with any of these.

A peasant with his crippled back and
        upright broom
dusting off the sun-gilded runway,
a banker's shouting ontic features
crabbed and tentacular,
        crabbed and tentacular.
Like everyone turns in on himself
I saw the gathered looped and spooking
out their children, these too
        stretched in their fire cavern,
talk would shift about the board
grinding thick lines of violence.
                Activity lights
flashed, cycles juddered to a pit reprieve
behind star-blasted rock
pooling oil.
                Still within a smoke scarf
three sit and talk and think to send a call
through wintery clearances.
Across the asphalt my bone vibrates.

Tap Tap.   Buzz.
                Calendar beetles
tap inside false ceilings,
        failing brands
collapse into the flickering of a hearth.
                Clear light annuls

red crackle, time-stamps every flash
expiring assets show in.
      Look, to make my call
      I found my mouth,
licked the barrier streaked with fuchsine,
          nibbled at the pith
between the tree and bark. Red daddy,
aren't I big enough to walk,
pick up my legs, my pace
      Look, I hack at overgrowth,
too grown up, well-fed for
jelly mould cars and download junket.
      Magenta freights a weary sky,
      heaved limbs abdicate.
Who hankers to walk grass and thrift.
Ankles pricked by gorse and heather.
Who walks on creases now shale
      pockmarked with spots of tar.
My ghost is trying its weight

on stepping stones, look, it's peeling off,
      weaned into the asphalt river.

Ahead I see this huge container.

Circular Quay

for Gig Ryan

You heard me. Don't pretend you didn't.
This town's foliage
corkscrews down from trees that sound
a bit off. Gentles in a neat layer
writhe like a pullover
over what at a distance looks
crisply modelled.
Up close, the scalloped sails pullulate
with air gusts writhing.
But of course you knew what I was
going to say and didn't have to pay heed.

Closeness cracks me up, it really does.
Eyes water and nostrils stream.
Buddleia brings butterflies across
the straits, and a sticky cloak of caterpillars
strips bark from dragon trees that weep
red blots.
Millions of bits of mirror
set in concrete beckon to the high cirrus.
No they don't. If we weren't so close
we'd have to face each other,
swarming across plenteous tiles.

Climate once mutual shrinks to its events.
Connectedness is
building a free state on pontoons
invisible from this wharf,
charging flakes of skin, fish scales
to overlay

paschal hordes showing up
obscurely furious. Words are spat
across the tresses of light breeze
a Koori boy puppets in, clothed
with tattoos of scabies spiralling at work.

I call him warrior and he trickles coin.
Here where paving is so thin if reticulated,
boots trouble the buried: re-
knit with aftershock as by the drop
of heavy fruit,
colonists paw at the straits high above.
They are wanting to shape up but
arise in glitter,
pegging out the foreshore in a seam
of gold studs. Take your hands
out of your pockets, stretch your arms.

Loss of Focus

in tribute to C.D. Wright

Appliqué of pale roses, appliqué of marigolds,
Golden cat's body thrusts up his neck and out
Expands a yawn, as if through an empty loupe
Casing through which unslowed flowers fell
Apart into petals, meeting no description, how
Could these be plucked and applied, how
Could hourglass stitches keep all pockets flush,
Left without capacity to hold a choked engine.

Toe down on a cracked paving stone to work.
Butterfly now colourless and just there, where
Is the pipette to lift its flutter and so carefully
Squeeze it down by the moan of a coal train,
Where the lens that hears, the pink saucer
Whose small aperture would titrate morning
And expand across the uncollective borders;
Light meter has gone missing and the light flat.

Airside

for Stephen Hayward, 1954–2015

Sewn across the settling scaled airways
    light collects passers-by,
passengers past thinking of, past
    never given a thought
slip between, pass quickly to other warmth.

    I had a turn.
A life rose and fell displayed through slats.
Detached smiles played.
Crowds of the dislodged block the terminal:

Was that a yellowhammer
tapping through dawn pipes?
A little bit of bread and no cheese
    broken above a camp?
        Trenchfoot and slow diarrhoea,
passless light scuffling between guy ropes.

    Stephen I had a turn.
Thick scents of tuberose, sketches of Spain.
Can our traipsing forward defy,
step by step, the terrible times?
    On the perimeter fence
bindweed turns to the flash of a departure.

Still Life

for Patrick Chamberlain

In early morning sun the made things
glow as though arising, as though labour
were fulfilled in a Tibetan shawl and in
black electronics. There cannot be a clean
break, the called-upon hold back, and
out of what they withhold release light.

Their withheld love flits on partitions,
shines showers, skedaddles over floors,
glancing guiltily, for what it rests upon
calls out. When it touches, its reserve
unbuttons, and a plastic bottle's dignity
calls back the sun that it might get cast.

Bring glow and shadow prone to marble,
object of love. Time and again ignored,
call turns to stone glinting so to taunt.
As an aside, as an aside a chubby hand
musses at the sky-blue drapery: foliage
recalls dancing light into its rigid gloss.

Sub Rosa

Face to face: this was not the face but the reverse
that looks himself in the eye: the dead eye
accusatory was a sty I'd been condemned to,
flares, lightning sheathed in white folds, neutered
and austere, so what beside, there's no such what
beside, but wallow in the clear.

This took a dim view, this took a pass, the orbit
broken out in spiffing stars dies against the cornea.
This was muscular, this was a thew, its impulsive
bladderdash caught on, let's skip the next part,
quickly break from where the subject interferes,
go straight to where light dies in the clear.

Come across the brick field to where rubbish
burns and the components pile up like dead eyes
graded by response to jets of expressed need.
Most wear masks behind their mobile faces
like sieves to catch the disconstruingly actual, so
filtering, record scrubbed, in the clear.

For I can see the lightning stitched on emptiness,
the satin swirls round one fork flicker, bunch
round a taut button, white folds it gathers back,
blank acceptance gets paraded like its thoughtful
counterpart, a pig-pen of indifference
a white constituent swanks from in the clear.

Face to face: this was not the face but the reverse,
yet taken for the face withheld, taken to transfer
wherever frailty permitted. Which is not meant,
but spattered as the punched-in settings of the
hard stars recuse them, the while I listen in
from this extension in the clear.

Nothing that I heard would tally. It was long love
point to point, the objects not their settings,
patching me face-forward. Time to clear.
The lode-star was the earth's entanglement,
lode I followed like magnetic tracks below
sheets of undifferentiated glossy matter.

Behind my eyes a dead pond gulps.
Behind my eyes a gas globe gets belched.
The world looks in upon this prodigal whose
tadpole transparent pink in its rescinded bubble
shakes on the verge of splitting off: let it go,
bounce across the fields, white and opaque.

Against Sleet

Between the booths a multiplicity fans and a shoal
of black limousines beyond each lane waits to carry
true appearances towards a match. Bricks are true
likewise in courses, body doubles wait
in absurd hats by the bus-stops. Enough. Modules
suffocate, and shall paving stones
                                        flip to release
crowds of the dead bent on disinterring keys or lost
combinations, seeking the digits stamped on one
brick among these sheer cliffs of acoustic control?
        They scrabble up
smooth walls, skin their alive knees and knuckles,
but will not get heard however loudly they cry out.

All shrivels in an instant, to less even than a dot,
two dots winking with an uttermost and desperate
desire to stay illuminated, for the ebbing fire to be
drawn by an intense draft of love, then a scratch
as of a flint and then a beach rattling with wet flint
for no scratch now can catch the sere ferns' fire;
pan to a mountainside marble offcuts litter,
slipping after blocks have been carted and ferried.

Some slip can be redemptive, scrape shins to bone,
and the sketchy reborn bash about in self-damage
patching and bruising their impeccable and light-
weight bodies, too lightweight to live.
        Fireflies
die disdained by these returning for the numbers
that might unlock their outline organs.

They scurry and they scrabble while the lone bleep
finishes its deathly ellipsis.
        Stars are fizzling out
above the shunting-yards, above the toll plazas,
above the reception facilities that check biometrics.
Two dots intensify and kindle on a flub of linen.

So the God decreed. All his answering compassion
brought to bear its breath on dots that flaring fade,
        would burst, would have to burst,
                as blossom bursts
between, along, across tiled boughs, horizoning
        embreezed, bursts on one look, its more
alert its signalling its pillow, nuzzled by a flying
fur the clouded sky is shaking loose
            tangling with the fragrant
brights, swirl of scent, an unimpeded joyous jostle.

Different Strokes

Different strokes do not tell the hours only,
    blows land on some vague heads,
a tillage starts their eyes and breaks
    across the conceptual landscape –
dense holts and hollows, brambles,
    scurryings and slither, outburst
of berries white to red to black to abstract.

Different strokes form the incline wanted,
    heart's true declivities, love's
configuration, rustling and whispering
    in thorn hollows, thick with non-
conceding but open to exchange,
    rather ventures so much in touch
there is no other but a velour admixture.

Different strokes do move a ball around,
    cartography of sunset, chart
the sea corresponds to. Feel ash smudge,
    feel smoke, warmth of elbow
as if touched by folded susurrus,
    breathing will take occupancy
of silhouettes that ache for this fulfilment.

Does concrete get more concrete once its
    clean edges crumble, once
competent plans digress from greyness,
    hatched parallels blur down –
does love once eroded by its own salts,
    moss mollifies, air acidulates,
lichen papers over, so become love more?

Different strokes humble the speech acts.

Or concrete most concrete in the abstract.

Storm Window

Venal or offhand, the sloppy event-scape,
    effusive faults heaped on all
sides and caught, kindled acts of terror;
    and the conspiratorial trusts
dredged living things, gouged amalgam.

A child envelope, secretive in its devices,
    crunched the stars for their
improvidence. In fact nothing gave but
    what was taken out to free
dead mechanism, feign flow of feeling.

Is that a destitute slip of truth? Through
    rubber seals securing storm
windows blew the tattered orphan scene –
    trees, cars, smashed boats, several
earlier visions of a dismantled skyscape.

It had played out differently in the last
    cottoning on. A healing process
kept the inner and outer face to face and
    subtle, intelligent boats bobbed
composed beneath the cloud-piled cliffs –

no, not a foggiest portent of the buckets,
    dehumidifiers, fluffy towels
sopping up orchestral cadenzas, brush-
    strokes streaming volubly be-
tween masonry and frame, these escape

when glass convulses to a tissue of pores
with valves blocked, a meadow
ploughs as clunch, windings spin madly,
chains of logic, articles of faith
go to smash through its vomiting panes.

Ways to Get about Busan

for Rod Mengham

Day awaits the kindly figures: will our visitors accept
proposals as once they did? Provocative zeroes float.
   Street parking sends the party-mad
   residents to their grid scales, for good –
   Admit One without limit of time.

On each surface aspect where the entertainment zone
lit up like a blush and stayed, short order overtaken
   brought a playlist, new attachments,
   mindful, other side of the coin,
   a temporal desert, its obverse aswarm.

In a moment a crease will plume cloud in concrete,
terminal beach, short squid, pails of slopping zeniths,
   sentiments that vaporise in perfume
   squalls, caprices of a passing shirt,
   no peg, no idol, focal point or polarity:

Could our visitors endure the abjection of constancy,
hand-held glare or touch screen that foams with poly-
   valent zeroes, pop-ups and events
   shimmering in light tied to fluctuations
   in Shanghai, saffron, silk trousseau?

They stagger in a pleater's shop amid clouds of steam,
the party leader will collapse blinded, their non-stop
   playlist runs on silent,
   dwelling cries from heaps of plans,
   look: this ground plan for a kitchen –

they will rely on lapses, dropouts twinkling and flaws,
losses pillowed what loss-bearers' loved foibles cast
    mocked under scrutiny, cherished bits
    injurious spurs grieve, a trilobite
    cricked neck hung weeping-on amidst

falbalas in their spun radish beds – the booster stage
nosed firmly on those left behind, force ready-ranked
    but yet unseated, shifting coloured
    beads, a regimen of spit and polish,
    aligning and then slotted brusquely

permanent packs in housings between bracket breves,
the anchorless, those who sidestep species and genus
    and just are. Squeals as property
    gets clamped, plaintive hoots resound
    with big data, red and gold flashes

pinned on for mating. Noise swirling in each amphora
between the ideograms of the actual, this is freedom,
    flushes stacks, retrieves such
    preferences which knowing best
    bring up a passenger pigeon:

visitors up to five like marked men were worrying out
inexplicable creases, peering through steam they scan
    ideograms perhaps sonic trace
    flash minatory above blank doors,
    crash calcified in a parking space,

splintering into layers of time a one-time meteor broke
in viruses, splinters of the true cross, the closed event
   capturing the icon with its
   dark hollow eyes it hoists
   for eternity in heaven's nave.

Disks will dawn above the bars still open all hours,
enamelled with a Pantone colour, semi-liquid bodies
   captured at high speed in varnish,
   processing in through-pass, print
   tokens, irises, electronic room keys,

rigid as medallions, wobbling into traffic-signal order.
What do these signify? Go back one step: the pleater
   can interpret a sidelong look,
   an eyebrow arches in a stroke thicket,
   through spurts of steam delivers

the last laughing owl to lips that outlined in pink coral
touch off a loudspeaker, no, an incompletely mapped
   heart-dithering trill, a living hand
   adjusts a lover's skew-whiff look,
   an earring through the steam, you!

guerdoned at the last with shame, riddle out the blots
of awful ash when gates to be hanged upon, bang shut,
   echo locked out of looped
   shunts, timed passes over, bends
   whose camber jolts kindly ones

off-course according to the manifest, our visitors take
      Look: Flash/ Look: Flash/ Look:
      actual blanks, blanks that in action
sift like ash but name what had been a tree. It is ash.
Would that it were an ash the palm still keeps in hand.
      A cedar in an anatomical snuff-box.

Branches have been populated, gaps filled with birds,
while underneath Building 40, eighty storeys high,

arguments of art shrivel in their cages, staggered trees
braced in metal, hunch in mist and micro-particles.

The effortful remembrances tinkle as an unavailing
bird pipes at the empire, against their wall of concrete

pre-moulded sections, rows of windows not lit up
as dusk falls. The blushing sky would divorce the day.

Stopover

When we shall be indigenous,
    dead soil dusting our birthday suits,
extruded without flaw, far from our home-to-be —
when we shall adopt for symbols
insects candying in lustrous pools
creeping out under
frozen food depositories,
        their thoraces
a diadem on the ancestral temple complex:

    When we shall be indigenous,
bitumen sanctioned, rhinoceros horn, horn of
stag beetle,
     indigenous to an airport with
all resident arrivals
fanning out boarding cards with priority access
        keeping our place
so we can state with assurance
This is our place. This is it.
       Wherever wherever:

When we shall be indigenous
hugging each other sweatily in the departure
decked with zigzags, like a Kwakina bowl,
    as though we inhabited
some spatial migraine,
digging ourselves into colour —
we shall have been indigenous, back in the day —

Back in the day there will have been only
this adjusted ridge, this wrinkle:

Everything will have been settled about a
bare twig and a single leafless bud
  No background:
Earth will have been what will be
light will have caught, in its own time:

And buzzing neither above, below, behind or
in any Wherever,
a bee of no particular calling, no stigma
brushing dust off its feet,
  soundlessly buzzes in wave-free space.

"The Savage is flying back home"
  blue not blue but a cobalt but glaucous
or turquoise but klein but teal/
   blue not blue will compose
a periphery. Possible
sky will accommodate the dust-clogged bee.
  When shall we be indigenous –
at length, at the end of the day, in fine,
  a twig, a bud, a bee,
enough that we fade into the cleft of the future –
when shall we once have been?

Speechless When It Comes to It

A beauty that case-hardens, keeps to its recess in theory
   Stretch fabric
               stone marquee –
And its husk once exhibited roils through a public lake
amidst water tulips, sails are hauled in, strong ceramic

greetings split themselves between sedimentary shelves
   attuned
to each carp generation. Nor only gloss, for saving such
beautiful, malignant capsule, broadcast to a listed wind,
           scuff only, wrinkled marge.

Bring down from the carrion sky and rise from greedy
earth to scrape along
   Rough stone agitates a single ear in place,
clodhoppers smash lenses as they trample
down the functional field. Come on now, do rise above.

Receding in the empyrean can such beauty still convert
parasol to stone, glancing such intention runs undefiled
sensorily,
   take it as it comes:
the station that sustains a systemic heart's tropes
         audible throughout the mass
   stays off-screen, dotted lines they recede also.

Go fly. Go shear. Go nautilus flotilla, go thin porcelain
finger-stalls, colour-cast, still lurching forward
for all the world a lake abstracts, switch shielded faces,
stinging eyes shut.

What avails
swarf collection magnetised to new-minted hull plying
fell dilapidation

shrugging off like teflon or stealth black whoever greet,
hopeful correspondents for this locked, eagle-pecked,
but in its shadow on the lungs
                    keeping overcast, this diagram –
butterknifes their past, a chastened shore with its future

splayed, heated, loving. Envy flitting carp knowing not
what avoidances animate their generations.
Stare down at your feet.
              Cut billows.
                    Shattered spume.
A shielded form cuts through sediment of smashed shell.

One–Nil

Had it but to bend inside a scorched stock frame,
     crouch until a fireball, kicked into touch,
flew into a goalmouth that flickers or a circus hoop,
and strikers and horses too dived for their portal –
     does this not hold a key to my jaw? –

Would such breakthrough be visual, visual only –
     down its silver guide-rails –
a global value chain driven towards the rocks –
plotting dies in flurries of simultaneity,
meteor trails banging around the spiral fuselage:

their bombardment will fall quiet in its time-lapse
cyclotron, played out by a bonfire of car tyres
licking at the long shot blocked by those tyre-shod –
     their kickabout taps in unifying
blackness the burning bloody heart of multiplicity –

for precedent has "a pretty Babe all burning bright"
in its firestorm sights/ a first-cut
merciful profession for its cauterising balm
blistering the hand of the grubby self whose flesh
hurts and hurts, identified once speed of light

resolves when suspended as a field of light, stacks
shots in sequence as the eye jumps from back to
glossy back across the circus ring – does each burst
finish in a fixture as it dies, did you not prepare
     chrome retractor clamps, is it irremediable

expulsion? If its purpose was to
punch a bullet through the skin drumhead – slam –
Had reparation but to bring about a perfect bending
course to an open goal, bloody gift of an open goal
sprays the red peristome or blazes fringe vision:

                Get stuck in –
                    Get forward –

            – is this particle therapy –
     – radiation shielding?
cross-section of a most effulgent mass?

Silent as Despairing Love

About such concealment all revolve
imagining its image.
Answer came there none. Force
of the unspoken circles the protected
as the sun warms slim purple
first fruits, coaxing the resin of
yet unestablished trees.

A wrinkled stone is made visible,
epitome of the sought-for,
while what rests obscure
pervades maturity, piling on flesh,
swaddling with its sweetness
what could not be touched so much
as englobed by a present promise

– whose date of expiry stares
out of a soft split. A nurseling image
under-ripe behind the lax
hooded eyes, steers by the dark
kernel with its
sway over time incommunicable,
held by a stone in its clasp,

gnarled as trees that over-fruit
teetering with swag,
big for the feast of worms and birds.
Their ripeness swaddles
convolutions; deep in the kernel,
a mere sliver, orchards are encoded,
lives condensed in one thought.

Air

Such was the air of her, air configures
clearings below trees, on memory's
sprung turf where summer sings and
pops like tinnitus shapes through larks
rising and falling –

voice on the telephone too, as shape
of her rising walk, shape of her room
décor, as in the air's decorum such
things were deftly articled to the room
memory scopes.

Smudged moon, smudged on a sharp
sky above a bearings factory. Smoke
stacks up. Oxygen contained
in cylinders clanks about a truck's cage,
air that has fallen

carries away, but still the air she had
round her shapes in a song's decorum,
bringing such things to mind, as who
ever will leap through ground hiss,
rattling glossy leaves?